CRICKET

GOODWILL PUBLISHING HOUSE™

B-3, Rattan Jyoti, 18 Rajendra Place,
NEW DELHI-110 008 (INDIA)
TEL.: 25750801, 25755519, 25820556 FAX : 91-11-25763428

ALL ABOUT
THE GAME OF
CRICKET

ISBN : 81-7245-358-2

Published by :

Rajneesh Chowdhry

GOODWILL PUBLISHING HOUSE™

B-3, Rattan Jyoti, 18 Rajendra Place,
NEW DELHI-110 008 (INDIA)
TEL.: 25750801, 25755519, 25820556 FAX : 91-11-25763428
E-Mail: goodwillpub@vsnl.net
Website: www.goodwillpublishinghouse.com

Printed at: Kumar Offset, Delhi.

Publisher's Note

The world is so large and mysterious that it is almost impossible to study each and every subject and identify the reason and logic beholding it. 'All About' is a series of illustrated books, designed to create awareness about such few subjects. The topics and subjects are related with your daily life, which have amazed us at times.

The series consists of books such as Feng Shui and Vaastu Shastra, which demonstrate the significance of directions in your life and the placement of objects, and house setting, from the Chinese and Indian perspective.

People with an inclination towards fortune telling have a lot to choose from, as the collection comprises of books ranging from Palmistry to Astrology to Numerology. Moreover, you can also analyse your Love and Star Signs.

All the health conscious people can get some handy health tips to keep fit. Moreover, the reader can learn about Yoga, to keep in shape. A few tips on Relaxation, Chakras, Tantric Sex, Reiki and Sex for Healing can provide you with helpful guidelines on how to relax after the day's work.

You can also learn all about the diseases that have enveloped the human race. The series provides all information on Diabetes, Diarrhoea, Constipation, Heart Attack, Kidney Stones, Anxiety, Typhoid, Hepatitis, Headache etc.

The series also mentions some of the most amazing and mystifying topics like Hypnosis, Face Reading, Body language and Magnetotherapy. To have a good tinkling experience the readers can enjoy some of the funniest jokes in the Joke Book. Further, you can also mobilize your brain cells in the book on Riddles.

Overall, 'All About' is an immense pool of information and facts that have always amused the living beings. It is an accumulation of the diverse, mysterious, realistic, day-to-day issues you always wanted to know about.

Contents

Introduction

Cricket is one of the most fascinating games of the modern times. The excitement and the enthusiasm is unmatched by any other sport. Originated by the British, the sport is now played throughout the world, particularly in Australia, India, Pakistan, South Africa, Sri Lanka, New Zealand and the West Indies. It has become the most prominent and famous game in the Indian subcontinent. Though cricket appears to be a simple game, it has various technical aspects. It requires a lot of concentration and patience. With years, the game has changed gradually and has improved technologically. This book provides the basic skills required to play the game and the correct way to play cricket. It also allows the reader to know the basic information required to be known by the budding players.

Basically, cricket is a game played with a ball and bat, between two teams of eleven players each. A formal game of cricket can last anything from an afternoon to several days. Although the game play and rules are very different, the basic concept of cricket is similar to that of baseball. Teams bat in successive innings and attempt to score runs, while the opposing team fields and attempts to bring an end to the batting team's innings. After each team has batted an equal number of innings (either one or two, depending on conditions chosen before the game), the team with the most runs wins.

CHAPTER 1

Origin

Cricket's origin is obscure. Evidence suggests it was played in England, in the 12th–13th century and was popular there by the end of the 17th century. The primitive bat was no doubt a shaped branch of a tree, resembling a modern hockey stick but considerably longer and heavier. The change to a straight bat was made to defend against length bowling, which had evolved with cricketers in Hambledon, a small village in Southern England. The bat was shortened in the handle and straightened and broadened in the blade, which led to forward play, driving, and cutting. As bowling technique was not very advanced during this period, batting dominated bowling, throughout the 18th century.

By the mid-18th century, the aristocracy had adopted the game. In 1744, the London Cricket Club produced what are noticeably the rules of modern cricket. The Melbourne Cricket Club (MCC), one of the oldest (1787) cricket organisations, is the game's international governing body.

Now in 2000, MCC has revised and re-written the Laws for the new Millennium. In this Code, the major innovation is the introduction of the Spirit of Cricket as a Preamble to the Laws.

CHAPTER 2

The Teams

A match is played between two teams, each of eleven players. The captain represents each team. Any one of the teams bats at one time while the other team fields. A coin is tossed at the beginning of the match to determine the team that would be batting first. The captain of the side winning the toss may elect to bat or field first.

All eleven players of the fielding team go out to field, and two players of the batting team go out to bat in the field. The remaining batting team waits, off the field for their turn to bat. Each batsman wears protective gear and carries a cricket bat.

The game progresses by the bowling of balls.

CHAPTER 3

Equipments

Cricket Ball:

A ball used in cricket is usually a hard, cork and string ball, covered with leather. A bit like a baseball (in size and hardness), but the leather covering is thicker and joined

in two hemispheres, not in a tennis ball pattern. The seam is thus like an equator, and the stitching is raised slightly. The circumference is between 224 and 229 millimetres (8.81 to 9.00 inches), and the ball weighs between 156 and 163 grams (5.5 to 5.75 ounces). Traditionally, the ball is dyed red, with the stitching left white. Nowadays white balls are also used, for visibility in games played at night under artificial lighting.

Cricket Bat:

The blade of the cricket bat is made up of willow, which is flat on one side, humped on the other for strength, attached to a sturdy cane handle. The blade has a maximum width of 108 millimetres (4.25 inches) and the whole bat has a maximum length of 965 millimetres (38 inches).

Wickets:

There are two wickets. The wickets are made up of wooden structures and consist of a set of three stumps topped by a pair of bails.

Stumps:

Stumps are three wooden posts, 25 millimetres (1 inch) in diameter and 813 millimetres (32 inches) high. They have spikes extending from their bottom end. Stumps are hammered into the ground in an evenly spaced row, with the outside edges of the outermost stumps 228 millimetres (9 inches) apart. This means they are just close enough together that a cricket ball cannot pass between them.

Bails:

Bails are two wooden crosspieces, which sit in grooves atop the adjacent pairs of stumps.

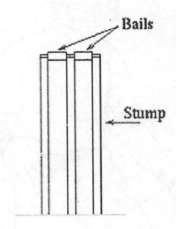

Protective Gear:

The protective gear is used by a batsman to protect him from injuries on the field. It is used to protect him against the ball. The protective gear includes pads, gloves, helmet, chest guard, leg guard etc.

Shoes:

The shoes are usually made up of leather, usually with spiked soles for grip on the grass.

Clothing:

The traditional dress code for the players has been long

pants, shirt (long or short sleeved depending on the weather), possibly a sleeveless or long-sleeved woolen pullover in cold weather. For games played with a red ball, the clothing must be white or cream. With a white ball, players usually wear uniforms in solid team colours. A hat or a cap is worn to keep the sun off. There are no regulations regarding identifying marks or numbers on clothing.

CHAPTER 4

The Field

A cricket field is a roughly elliptical field of flat grass, ranging in size from about 90 to 150 metres (100-160

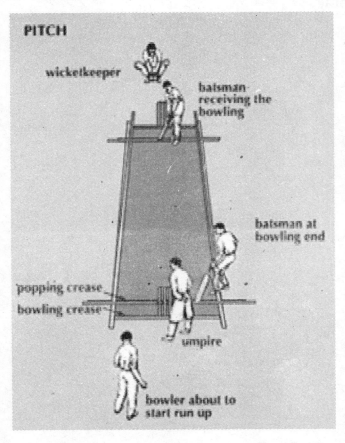

PITCH

wicketkeeper

batsman receiving the bowling

batsman at bowling end

popping crease

bowling crease

umpire

bowler about to start run up

yards) across, bounded by an obvious fence or other marker. There is no fixed size or shape for the field, although large deviations from a low-eccentricity ellipse are discouraged. In the centre of the field, and usually aligned along the long axis of the ellipse, is the pitch, a carefully prepared rectangle of closely mown and rolled grass over hard packed earth. It is marked with white lines, called creases.

There are two type of creases. One is the batting crease from where batsman bats and other is for a bowler to bowl, called bowling or popping crease. It is 8 feet 8 inches in length (or 2.64m), and the stumps are in the centre.

CHAPTER 5

The Play

The fielding team consisting of eleven players comes to field, with two players from batting side to bat. Other players of batting team wait for their turn. Batsman puts on his protective gear and holds a cricket bat. The order in which the teams bat is determined by a coin's toss. The captain of the side winning the toss may elect to bat or field first.

All eleven players of the fielding team go out to field, two players of the batting team go out to bat. The remaining batting team waits off the field for their turn to bat. Each batsman wears protective gear and carries a cricket bat.

The game begins by the bowling of balls. The sequence of events which constitutes a ball follows:

The fielding team disperses around the field to positions assigned to them by the captain. Their role is to stop runs being scored and to get batsmen out. One fielder is the *bowler*. He takes the ball and stands some distance behind one of the wickets (i.e. away from the pitch). Another fielder is the *wicket-keeper*, who wears a pair of webbed gloves designed for catching the ball and protective pads covering the shins. He squats behind the opposite wicket. The rest of the fielders have no special equipment. Gloves to assist catching the ball are not allowed to anyone, but the wicket-keeper.

One batsman stands behind each popping crease, near a wicket. The batsman farthest from the bowler is the *striker*, and the other is the *non-striker*. The striker stands before his wicket, on or near the popping crease, in the batting stance.

The batsman stands with his bat held down in front of the wicket, ready to hit the ball, which is bowled from the

other end of the pitch. The batsman usually rests the lower
end of the bat on the pitch and then taps the bat on the

pitch a few times as 'warm-up' backswings.

The non-striker simply stands behind the other popping crease, waiting to run if necessary. The bowler takes a run-up from behind the non-striker's wicket. He passes to one side of the wicket, and when he reaches the non-striker's popping crease, he bowls the ball towards the striker, usually bouncing the ball once on the pitch before it reaches the striker.

The striker may then attempt to hit the ball with his bat. If he misses it, the wicket-keeper catches it and the ball is completed. If he hits it, the two batsmen may score runs by running to other ends. When the runs are completed, the ball is also considered completed. The ball is considered to be in play from the moment the bowler begins his run-up. It remains in play until any of several above mention conditions occur, after which it is called *dead*. The ball is also dead if it lodges in the striker's clothing or equipment. Once the ball is dead, it is returned to the bowler for the next *delivery* (another name for the bowling of a ball). Between deliveries, the batsmen may leave their creases and confer with each other.

When one bowler has completed six balls, it is the end of an *over*. A different member of the fielding team is given the ball to bowl the next over. He bowls the next over from the opposite end of the pitch. The batsmen do not change ends, so the roles of striker and non-striker swap after each over. Any member of the fielding team can

bowl. However, a bowler is not allowed to deliver two consecutive overs. Once a bowler begins an over, he must complete it, unless he is injured or suspended during the over.

Another possibility during a ball is that a batsman may get *out*.

If a batsman gets out, the ball is dead immediately, so it is impossible to get the other batsman out from the same ball. The batsman, who is out leaves the field, and the next batsman in the team comes in to bat. The *not out* batsman remains on the field. The order in which batsmen come in to bat in an innings is not fixed. The team captain may change the batting order at any time, and the order does not have to be the same in each innings.

When ten batsmen are out, no new batsmen remain to come in, and the innings is completed with one batsman remaining not out. The roles of the teams then change, and the team, which fielded first, get to bat through an innings. When both teams have completed the agreed number of innings, the team, which has scored the most runs, wins.

CHAPTER 6

Scoring Runs

There are many ways of getting runs. However, the batsmen in the team do the scoring. Whenever a batsman hits the ball during a delivery, he may score runs.

A run is scored by the batsmen running between the popping creases. When they both reach the opposite crease, one run is scored, and they may return for another run immediately. The number of times they cross each other, a run is added to the team's account. The fielding side attempts to prevent runs being scored by threatening to *run out* one of the batsmen.

If the batsmen are attempting to take runs, and a fielder gathers the ball and hits a wicket with it, dislodging one or both bails, while no batsman is behind that wicket's popping crease, then the nearest batsman is run out. Specifically, the batsman must have some part of his body or his bat (provided he is holding it) grounded behind (not on) the crease.

The batsmen carry their bats as they run, and turning for another run is accomplished by touching the ground beyond the crease with an outstretched bat. The batsmen do not have to run at any time they think it is unsafe. It is a common practice to hit the ball and elect not to run.

If the batsmen run one or three (or five! rare, but possible), then they have swapped ends and their striker/non-striker roles are reversed for the next ball (unless the ball just completed is the end of an over).

In addition to scoring runs like this, if a batsman hits the

ball so that it reaches the boundary fence, he scores four
runs, without needing to actually run them. If a batsman
hits the ball over the boundary on the full, he scores six
runs. If a four or six is scored, the ball is completed and
the batsmen cannot be run out. If a spectator encroaches

on to the field and touches the ball, it is considered to have reached the boundary. If a fielder gathers the ball, but then steps outside or touches the boundary while still holding the ball, four runs are scored. If a fielder catches the ball on the full and, either during or immediately after the catch, steps outside or touches the boundary, six runs are scored.

The batsmen usually stop taking runs when a fielder is throwing the ball back towards the pitch area. If no fielder near the pitch gathers the ball and it continues into the outfield again, the batsmen may take more runs. Such runs are called *overthrows*. If the ball reaches the boundary on an overthrow, four runs are scored in addition to the runs taken before the overthrow occurred.

Runs scored by a batsman, including all overthrows, are credited to him by the scorer. The number of runs scored by each batsman is an important statistic.

If, while running multiple runs, a batsman does not touch the ground beyond the popping crease before he returns for the next run, then the umpire at that end usually signals *one short*, and the number of runs scored is reduced by one.

Like all other games, umpire's decision is final. It is not argued by any of the players on the field.

CHAPTER 7

Types Of Dismissals

There are numbers of ways for a batsman to get out. A bowler can dismiss the batsman out in various ways, provided he gets the consent of the umpire.

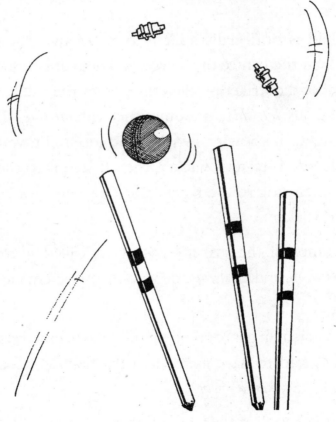

A batsman can get out only if the wicket is said to be *broken*, and if one or both the bails have been dislodged and fallen on the ground. If the bails have fallen off for any reason and the ball is still in play, then breaking the wicket must be accomplished by pulling a stump completely out of the ground. If the wicket needs to be broken like this with the ball, the uprooting of the stump must be done with the ball in contact with the stump.

The field is notionally split into two halves, along a line down the centre of the pitch. The half of the field in front of the striker is called the *off side*, the half behind is called the *leg side*, or sometimes the *on side*. Thus, standing at the bowler's wicket and looking towards a right-handed striker's wicket, the off side is to the left and the leg side to the right (and vice-versa for a left-handed striker).

The stumps of the striker's wicket are called *off stump*, *middle stump*, and *leg stump*, depending on which side they are on.

When a batsman gets out, no matter by what method, his wicket is said to have *fallen*, and the fielding team are said to have *taken a wicket*.

Let's have a look at the ways of getting out:

Caught:

A batsman is declared caught if a fielder catches the ball on the full after the batsman has hit it with his bat. However, if the fielder touches or over steps the boundary after catching the ball the batsman scores six runs and is not out.

Bowled:

A batsman is bowled if he misses the ball with his bat and it hits and breaks the wicket directly from the bowler's delivery. It does not matter whether the batsman is in front or behind his popping crease. He is also out bowled if the ball breaks the wicket after deflecting from his bat or body. The batsman is not out if the bails do not fall on the ground even if ball hits the stumps.

Leg Before Wicket:

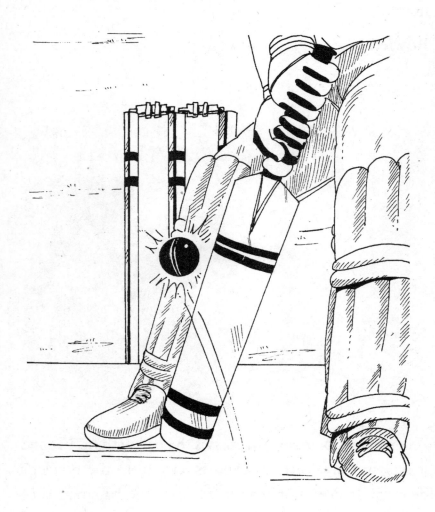

A batsman is declared leg before wicket if the batsman misses the ball with his bat, but intercepts it with part of his body when it would otherwise have hit the wicket. It is probably the most difficult judgment for the umpire. An umpire must adjudicate such a decision, and will only do so if the fielding team appeals to the umpire. A bowler generally shouts *Howzzat?* (How's that?), usually quite enthusiastically and loudly. If the ball bounces outside an imaginary line drawn straight down the pitch from the outside edge of leg stump, then the batsman cannot be out LBW, no matter whether or not the ball would have hit the stumps. If the batsman attempts to play a shot at the ball with his bat (and misses) he may only be given

out LBW if the ball strikes the batsman between imaginary lines drawn down the pitch from the outside edges of leg and off stumps (i.e. directly in line with the wicket). If the batsman does not attempt to play the ball with his bat, then he may be given out LBW without satisfying this condition, as long as the umpire is convinced the ball would have hit the wicket. If the ball has hit the bat before the hitting the batsman, then he cannot be given out LBW.

Stumped:

A batsman is stumped if he misses the ball while

attempting to play the ball, steps outside his crease, and the wicket-keeper gathers the ball and breaks the wicket with it, before the batsman can ground part of his body or his bat behind his crease. A batsman usually gets out this way when the bowler is a spinner or a slow bowler

Run Out:

A batsman is run out if he is attempting to take a run, or to return to his crease after an aborted run, and a fielder breaks that batsman's wicket with the ball while he is out of the crease. The fielder may either break the wicket

with a hand, which holds the ball, or with the ball directly.
It is possible for the non-striker to be run out if the striker
hits the ball straight down the pitch towards the non-
striker's wicket, dettected by the bowler on to the wicket
while the non-striker is out of his crease. If the ball is hit
directly on to the non-striker's wicket, without being
touched by a fielder, then the non-striker is not out. If the
non-striker leaves his crease (to take a run) while the
bowler is running up, the bowler may run him out without
bowling the ball. Batsmen cannot be run out while the
ball is dead - so they may confer in the middle of the pitch
between deliveries if they desire.

Handling The Ball:

A batsman is out in this way if the batsman touches the
ball with a hand not currently holding the bat, without
the permission of the fielding side. This does not include
being hit on the hand by a delivery, or any other non-
deliberate action.

Obstructing The Field:

A batsman is given out by the umpire in this way if he
deliberately interferes with the efforts of fielders to gather
the ball or effect a run out. This does not include running
on the path between the fielder and the wicket so that
the fielder cannot throw the stumps down with the ball,

which is quite legal, but does include any deliberate attempt to swat the ball away.

Hit The Ball Twice:

A batsman is declared out if he hits a delivery with his bat and then deliberately hits the ball again for any reason other than to defend his wicket from being broken by the ball. If the ball bounces or rolls around near the stumps, the batsman is entitled to knock it away so as to avoid being bowled, but not to score runs.

Timed Out:

A batsman is also given out if he takes longer than two minutes to arrive at the crease after the previous batsman has been given out.

If a batsman is out caught, bowled, LBW, stumped, or hit wicket, then the bowler is credited with taking the wicket. No single person is credited with taking a wicket if it falls by any other method.

Hit Wicket:

A batsman is declared hit wicket if he breaks the wicket while attempting to hit a ball or taking off for a first run. This includes with the bat or dislodged pieces of the batsman's equipment - even a helmet or spectacles!

CHAPTER 8

Officials

The game of cricket is adjudicated by two umpires, who make all decisions on the field and whose word is absolutely final. One umpire stands behind the non-striker's wicket,

ready to make judgments on LBWs and other events requiring a decision. The other umpire (called leg umpire) stands in line with the striker's popping crease, about 20 metres (20 yards) to one side (usually the leg side, but not always), ready to judge stumpings and run-outs at his end. The umpires remain at their respective ends of the pitch, and exchange positions after every over.

In modern times, a third umpire is sometimes used to make decisions. He sits off the field, with a television replay monitor. If an on-field umpire is unsure of a decision concerning either a run out or a stumping attempt, he may signal for the third umpire to view a television replay. The third umpire views a replay, in slow motion if necessary, until he either reaches a decision or decides that he cannot make a clear decision. He signals the result to the on-field umpire, who then summons the rule to the batsman. If the equipment fails, the replay umpire signals no decision. The replay umpire is commonly used for deciding run outs and stumpings.

Whenever any decision is doubtful, the umpire usually rules it in the favour of the batsman.

If the ball hits an umpire, it is still live and play continues. If it lodges in an umpire's clothing, then it is dead.

The game is presided over by a *match referee*, who is

appointed to see that the match is played in the right spirit and under the designed rules. He watches the proceedings from outside the field. The referee makes no decisions of relevance to the outcome of the game, but

determines penalties for breaches of various rules and misconduct. In professional games, these penalties are monetary fines. They may include banning of certain players as well.

Arguing with an umpire's decision is a major offence on the field. Anything more than a polite question to the umpires is heavily frowned upon and can attract a penalty from the referee. The most serious misconduct in a cricket match is of the order of a rude gesture to an opponent or throwing the ball into the ground in disgust. Such gross misbehaviour can attract large fines and possibly match suspensions. Penalties for physical violence can only be guessed at, but would possibly be a career suspension. However, the match referee tries that the player is not penalised heavily.

CHAPTER 9

Extras

Extras are the runs that are not scored by the batsman but are either given away by the mistake of a bowler or collected by the batsman in some other way. In this case, the batsman does not hit the ball. Extras are not credited

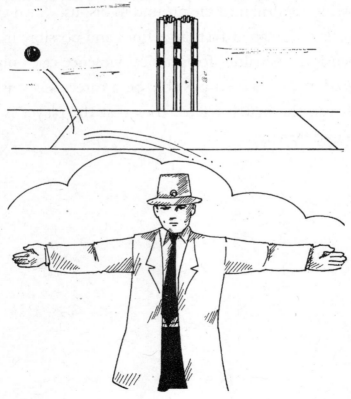

to any batsman, and are recorded by the scorer separately. The total number of runs for the innings is equal to the sums of the individual batsmen's scores and the extras. There are four types of extras: *no balls, wides, byes, and leg byes*.

As per the rules of cricket a bowler must bowl each ball with part of his frontmost foot behind the popping crease. If he oversteps this mark, he bowls a *no ball*. The umpire is very alert in the field and calls it a 'no ball' immediately in a loud voice. The batsman may play and score runs as usual, and may not be out by any means except run out, handle the ball, hit the ball twice, or obstructing the field.

Further, if the batsman does not score any runs from the ball, one run is added to the batting team's score. Also, the ball reaches the boundary, four byes (of the appropriate type) are scored.

CHAPTER 10

The Bowling Action

As per the ICC (International Cricket Council), the bowling action itself has to conform to several restrictions.

The guidelnes say that the bowler's arm must be straight, when the ball is bowled (so no 'throwing' is allowed). The ball must be bowled over arm, and not underarm. There is a difference between 'bowling' and 'throwing'. When a player throws the ball, the elbow is cocked and used to impart energy to the ball by straightening. When a ball is bowled, the elbow joint is held extended throughout. All the energy is imparted by rotation of the arm about the shoulder, and possibly a little by wrist motion. For a right-handed bowler, the action goes roughly as follows:

After the run-up, the right foot is planted on the ground with the instep facing the batsman. The right arm extends backwards and down at this stage. The left foot comes down on the popping crease as the bowler's momentum carries him forward - he stands essentially left-side on to the batsman. As the weight transfers to the left foot, the right arm is brought over the shoulder in a vertical arc. The ball releases near the top of the arc, and the follow-through brings the arm down and the right shoulder forward rapidly.

Bouncing the ball on the pitch is not mandatory. It's usually done because the movement of the ball off the pitch makes it much harder to hit. Un-bounced deliveries, or *full tosses* are usually easy to play and the batsman usually dispatches it to the boundary. The bowler usually bowls these deliveries unintentionally. A full toss above waist height is a no ball,

and an umpire who suspects that such a ball was deliberate will give the bowler an official warning. A warning is also given if the umpire believes the bowler is bowling at the body of a batsman in a deliberate attempt to injure the batsman. After two warnings a bowler is restricted from bowling for the rest of the innings.

If any rule governing the bowling action is violated, a no ball results.

Bowlers are allowed to polish the ball by rubbing it with cloth (usually on their trouser legs) and applying saliva or sweat to it. Any other substance like a cream or polish is illegal, as is rubbing the ball on the ground. Usually one side of the ball is polished smooth, while the other wears, so that the bowler can *swing* the ball (curving the ball through the air). It is also illegal to roughen the ball by

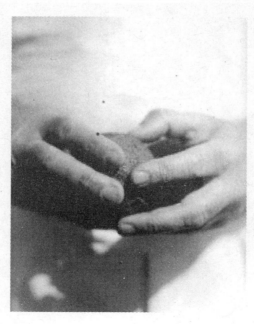

any means, including scraping it with the fingernails or lifting the seam. A bowler who illegally tampers with the ball is immediately suspended from bowling for the rest of that innings.

The bowler is allowed to bowl from either side of the wicket as per his will, but must inform the umpire and the batsmen if he wants to change sides. Bowling with the bowling arm closest to the wicket is called *over the wicket*, and is most common. Bowling with the non-bowling arm closest to the wicket is called *around the wicket*.

The bowler may abort his run-up or not let go of the ball if he loses his balance or timing for any reason. The umpire signals it as a dead ball and the ball must be bowled again. If a bowler loses his grip on the ball during the delivery action, it is considered to be a live ball only if it is propelled forward of the bowler. If such a ball comes to rest in front of the striker, but any distance to the side, the striker is entitled to walk up to the ball and attempt to hit it with his bat. The fielding team is not supposed to touch the ball until the striker either hits it or declines to do so.

A delivery may also be aborted if the striker steps away from his stumps, if he is distracted. An insect or dust may distract him.

CHAPTER 11

Fielding Positions

Field placements in cricket are not standardised but there are traditional positions that can be viewed for major part of the match. There are several named field positions, and

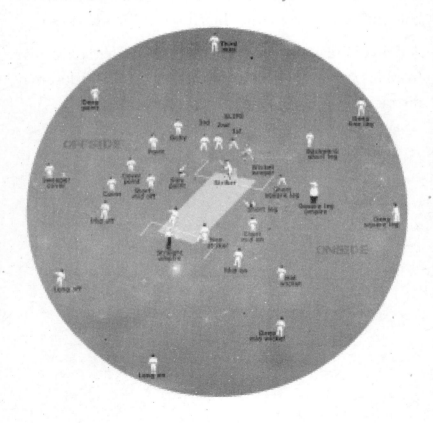

the fielding captain uses different combinations of them for tactical reasons, as per the situation of the match. There are also further descriptive words to specify variations on the positions labelled by simple names, so that any position in which a fielder stands can be described.

Description of field positions

Wicket-keeper:

Wicket-keeper is the most crucial position behind the stumps, in modern day cricket. He stands right behind the stumps, ball after ball. His main responsibility is to catch the ball that comes his way. He plays a vital role in the dismissal of the batsmen behind the wicket. He plays a significant role in saving runs behind the wicket and effecting run outs. Wicketkeeper is in a right position to analyse both the batsmen and bowlers. It is a very hectic job and requires a lot of athleticism and concentration. With fast bowling dominating most of the attacks, a wicketkeeper can easily make or spoil the outcome of a match. Apart from the alertness to hold fine snicks and uncanny bouncers, he also has to stop giving additional runs in the form of byes. A wicketkeeper also has to take split second decisions especially when trying to go for a catch in the direction of the slips.

First slip:

First slip is a vital position and he stands to the right of the wicketkeeper for a right-handed batsman and vice versa for the left-handed batsman. The first slip has is a specialised catching position and he has to adept in art of catching bare handed. The first slip plays a major role, when the ball is new and swinging. The fast bowlers extract bounce and swing in the first few overs, when the ball is new. He has to be very alert at such moments. The fielder at first slip normally stands a few paces behind the wicketkeeper as the ball tends to travel very fast if a batsmen snicks a fast bowler. The fielder at first slip has to coordinate well with wicketkeeper to ensure that he gets the right snicks. A fielder with quick reflexes and alertness is usually preferred at such a position. He has to be very alert when the spinner is bowling, as he has to read the turn well. At one point of time it was considered as the best position for a

player to relax. With more emphasis on Limited Overs cricket and fast bowling, the player at first slip really has a job on hand.

Second slip:

The fielder at second slip is to the right of the first slip position and the wicketkeeper for a right-handed batsman and vice versa for a left-handed batsman. But, in physical positioning, the second slip is more or less aligned with the wicketkeeper. The second slip is generally employed on a long-term basis in Test matches. In the One-Day Internationals, genuine fast bowlers may employ the second slip as they anticipate snicks from the batsmen who would like to open the face of the bat and glide the ball. The second slip has to have good reflexes as well as alertness.

Third slip:

Third slip is another important member of the slip cordon. He is as responsible as his two other counterparts. The fast bowlers usually prefer him. This position again is to the right of the second slip and a step ahead of the wicketkeeper in case of a right-handed batsman and vice versa for the left-handed batsman. Fast bowlers and the medium pacers normally employ third slip in Test matches, when the ball is new.

Fourth slip:

It's a necessity for fast bowlers of high quality. It is not necessary there all the time and is rarely seen in the matches. However, it is very uncommon in the One-Day Internationals. Great fast bowlers of past and present have utilised this position very well to their effect. The fourth slip also stands to the right of the wicket-keeper when there is a right-handed batsman.

Gully:

The gully is to the right of the slip cordon and covers the area just square of the wicket on the off side. It is also a catching position and its motive is to encourage the

batsman to go for the slash. The fielder at gully is usually the most agile of all the players who can dive well and have a good sense of anticipation.

Third man:

Third man is positioned at the boundary line right behind the slip cordon. The fielder at third man has to cover a

vast area in the outfield. The fielder at third man is also required to have a strong arm as he may sometimes have to hurl the ball from the boundary line to the wicketkeeper in one quick action. This can be an ideal place for fast bowlers to get back their breath in between overs like any deep fielding position.

Silly point:

Silly point is a specialised catching position generally employed in the test matches. The silly point is placed in front of the wicket on the off side. The fielder is almost within handshaking distance of the batsmen. The idea of silly point is to put additional pressure on the batsmen and make him pop the ball in the air so that he gets an opportunity to catch the ball. This position assumes special significance for spinners as a lot of bat-pad catches may go in that direction. The fielder at silly point has to show a remarkable reflex action and the fielder should also possess guts and courage to stand there.

Point:

It is probably the most important position in the field. Usually the best fielder in the side can be seen at this position. Point is located is exactly at 90 degrees to the batsman. This position requires the fielder to show a lot of anticipation. The fielder at this position invariably

charges at the batsman and has to keep an eye for the hard square drives. Jonty Rhodes of South Africa is renowned for this position.

Cover point:

It is a vital position on the off side in front of the wicket. This is the area in which batsmen normally drive through with the full flow off the bat and hence fielders at this position have to be extra alert. The position is between point (square off the wicket) and cover, hence the name cover point.

Deep point:

Deep point is placed at the boundary line on the off side. It Is basically a defensive position. The fielder at deep point is usually right behind the point fielder and he needs to have a good arm as he has to throw the ball back to the wicket-keeper. The basic idea of this position is to prevent the batsmen from scoring boundaries. Sometimes a fielder at square third man can also man the deep point boundary, but has to do a fair amount of running to reach the ball.

Cover:

The fielder at cover is stationed to the right of point and has to anticipate the movement of the ball from the movements of the bat. It is a position, where the ball can come with blinding speed on the up.

Extra cover:

It is an additional position in front of the wicket. A captain can opt for cover and extra cover when he wants to have a strong off side field. Similar to that of cover, the extra cover fielder is a little to the right and more in line with the 'V' of the batsman's stroke.

Short mid off:

A short mid-off is placed quite close to the batsman. It is not like the silly point but a little further away from that.

One needs to have safe pair of hands to field at this position. The position is almost midway to the wicket from the batting crease.

Mid off:

Mid off is a position on the off side for almost straight in line with the bat. It is placed to protect the straight drives and one has to be alert. It is an ideal position

for the captains to analyse the position and the proceedings of the game.

Sweeper cover:

It is another defensive position along the boundary rope similar to the deep point. The fielder at this position needs to have a good arm and good stamina to run around in the field. In fact, the sweeper cover position is an outcome of Limited Overs Internationals, where the fielding sides decide to keep the runs to the bare minimum.

Long off:

Long off is a defensive position in the deep, on the off side. The fielder at long off is behind the mid off and has to cover a fairly substantial area from the sightscreen to the sweeper cover position and beyond. As in any deep position, the fielder at long off is required to have a safe pair of hands. The fielder also needs to be alert as well as very good thrower of the cricket ball.

Long on:

This position is an exact mirror image of long off on the on side of the wicket. The area of coverage for a long on fielder will go up to deep midwicket and beyond.

Mid on:

This is another position almost straight of the batsman and in some ways similar to the mid off position. This is another position from which captains can judge the situation of the game.

Mid wicket:

Mid wicket is placed on the on side and he has a lot work to do against wristy batsmen. A fielder at mid wicket has to be extra alert as any bad ball down the leg side or short pitched delivery will leave this area open for vulnerability.

Deep mid wicket:

Deep mid wicket is placed at the boundary line on the on side. The fielder at deep mid wicket also has to be careful while judging skiers.

Short mid on:

A position more or less similar to the short mid off, but on the on side.

Forward short leg:

It is a specialised position for catching on the on side. This has become one area of great specialisation with some fielders training to stand in this position. One needs to have a great sense of anticipation to field here. This position is of utmost importance in the longer version of the game, when the batsman has more defensive approach.

Short square leg:

A position to the right of forward square leg. This used to be very popular, when the Indian spinners were on a song.

Backward short leg:

This position is similar to first slip on the leg side and is very often referred to as leg slip. Again a position used when spinners are in operation, the fielder at backward square leg needs to show a good sense of judgment and anticipation.

Square leg:

This position is square of the wicket on the on side almost in line with the batting crease.   This is also the position for the leg umpire. It prevents the batsman from going for uppish pull shots. The fielder at square leg needs extra caution, when fast bowlers are in operation. A mistimed hook or pull shot can result in a catch to the square leg region.

Deep/ backward square leg:

This position is usually adopted by fast bowlers to tempt the batsmen into the hook shot. This is region can also be monitored by the fielders from the deep mid wicket and deep fine leg regions.

Fine leg:

This position is fine on the leg side to the right of the square leg region. A traditional position, where fast bowlers generally relax in between overs.

Deep fine leg:

This is a position on the leg side and almost behind the wickets. The role of a fielder at this position is essentially to cut off boundaries. As the region between deep square leg and deep fine leg is manned by a fielder on the boundary line, he will have to do a lot of hard work in case of fine flicks down the leg side.

CHAPTER 12

Substitutions

In case a player suffers a serious injury and is unable to continue with the play, a substitute can replace him. Substitutes can replace any number of fielders. A substitute

is only allowed to field - he is not allowed to bowl, nor can he bat. A substitute is also not allowed to keep wickets. A substituted player must return to the field as soon as the replaced player is able to resume playing without danger.

If a batsman is injured, he can retire and resume his innings when he is fit to play again, so long as his team's innings is not over. If a batsman is too injured to bat when no other batsmen remain to come in after a wicket falls, his innings must be forfeited and his team's innings ends. If a batsman is able to bat, but not run, he can get a runner for himself. A runner may be any of the players of the playing eleven except the non-striker. The runner must wear the same equipment as the batsman, and run for him as per his will. The injured non-runner must remain behind his crease all times when the ball is in play or risk being run out, even if his runner is safely behind a crease.

If a bowler is injured during an over and cannot complete it, another bowler must bowl the remaining deliveries in that over. The bowler chosen to finish the over must not be the bowler who bowled the previous over, and must not bowl the over immediately following either.

A player is not allowed to leave the field for injury unless the injury is sustained on the field. An injured player who takes the field may not leave because of his pre-existing injury, unless it is clearly aggravated further on the field.

CHAPTER 13

Umpire's Signals

The umpires signal various events with gestures, as follows:

Out:

When a batsman is out, the umpire indicates the decision by raising one hand above his head, with the index finger extended.

Not Out:

The umpire usually shakes his head or may not signal anything at all.

Four:

The umpire signals four by extending his arm horizontally and waves briefly back and forth in a horizontal arc.

Six:

The umpire signals a six by raising both arms straight over the head.

No Ball:

To indicate a no ball, the umpire holds an arm out horizontally.

wide:

The umpire holds both arms out horizontally to signal a wide.

Byes:

The umpire signals byes by raising one arm over the head with his palm open.

Leg Byes:

The umpire signals leg byes by raising one leg and tapping the knee with one hand.

Dead Ball:

If the umpire has to signal dead ball to prevent the players from assuming that the ball is still alive, he waves both arms across each other in front of his abdomen.

One Short:

One short is signalled by touching the tip of one hand to the same shoulder.

TV Replay:

With the assistance of technology, the umpire can use the third umpire to make a decision based on a TV replay. The umpire on the field signals by drawing a large square shape in the air with both hands, spreading them out

high in the air in front of him, bringing them down, and
then together again.

CHAPTER 14

The Two Forms Of Cricket

There are two versions of cricket. The first is limited duration, in which a specific number of hours of playing time are allocated and each team plays two innings.

The second is limited overs, in which each team play one innings each of a fixed number of overs.

First Class Cricket

First class cricket matches are the most prestigious traditional games, played at a professional level. The top-level games are international *Test matches*, played between two countries. There are usually test series between two countries. The *Ashes* is the traditional test series played between Australia and England since years. There are also domestic first class cricket competitions. First class matches are of limited duration.

Test matches are played within five days, with six hours of play everyday. Each day's play is divided into three *sessions* of two hours each with a 40-minute lunch break between the first two sessions for lunch, and a 20 minute tea break between the last two sessions. A short drinks break is taken every hour, or more often in very hot weather. Play usually begins at 11:00 local time and goes up to 18:00, although this may be varied if sunset occurs early. The scheduled close of playtime is called stumps. Test matches are never played under artificial lighting.

Each team plays two innings. Each team bats twice and also fields twice unless a team wins by an innings. They are played in alternating order. Each innings is over when either ten batsmen are out, or the captain of the batting side *declares* the innings closed. When all the innings are completed, the team that scores more runs wins. If there is a tie, the result stands

---

Score Board

		1st Innings
Australia		435
England		384
		2nd Innings
Australia		80
	Wkts	0
Batsman	1	52
	2	22
Extras		6

If by the end of the final day's play, the team is unable to win, the game is a draw, no matter who appeared to be "winning". Thus the strategic importance of sometimes declaring an innings closed, in order to have enough time to dismiss the other team and so win the game.

The order of the innings alternates except when the **follow-on** is enforced. This can occur if the second team to bat in the first innings scores 200 or more runs less than the first team. The captain of the first team may then ask the second team to follow on, i.e. to bat its second innings immediately, and defer his own team's second innings until afterwards.

Whenever a change of innings occurs during a session, a ten minute break is taken. If the end of an innings occurs within ten minutes of the end of the first or second sessions, the ten-minute break is lost and the scheduled interval is shifted to begin immediately. If the end of an innings occurs within ten minutes of stumps, the day's play ends early.

Test matches are played with a red cricket ball. A new ball is used for the beginning of each innings. The same ball must be used throughout the innings, being replaced only in the following cases:

1. The captain of the bowling team may elect to take a new ball at any time after 80 overs have been bowled

with the previous ball.

2. If the ball is lost, it is replaced.

3. If the ball is damaged, either by the stitching coming

undone or the ball becoming clearly non-spherical, it is
replaced.

In cases 2 and 3, the ball must be replaced by a previously
used ball of similarly worn condition to the old ball, as
chosen by the umpires. If the ball is ever hit so that a
spectator gathers it, the spectator must return it so that
play can continue.

On each day of play in a Test match, a minimum of 90
overs must be bowled. If the bowling team has not bowled
the required minimum by the scheduled stumps time, play
is extended until the required number of overs have been
bowled. Whenever an innings ends, the number of overs
to be bowled is recalculated, disregarding the number of
overs bowled so far during the same day. The required
minimum is calculated to be the number of minutes of
play remaining, divided by 4 and rounded up. On the last
day of play, this formula is used up until one hour before
stumps, then fifteen overs are added to the result. If extra
overs are bowled before the time one hour before stumps
on the final day, then there still must be a minimum of
fifteen overs bowled after the time one hour before stumps.
All of these conditions are recalculated for time lost due
to poor weather, at a rate of one over per 4 minutes of
lost time. If a day's play ends early because of poor weather
conditions, all calculations are reset for the next day.

If there is heavy cloud cover, the umpires may decide that the light level is too low for the play. In that case, they

offer the light to the batsmen, who may agree to leave the field or may decide to play on. If the light deteriorates further, the umpires offer again. If the batsmen decide to leave the field and the light improves, the umpires make the decision to resume play.

If a fielder leaves the field for any reason and then returns during the same innings, he is not supposed to bowl until he has been on the field again for as much time as he spent off the field.

Test matches are played in Series between two of the official Test nations. A Test Series consists of a set number of matches, from one to six, all of which are played to completion, even if one team gains an unbeatable lead in the Series. Series of three or five matches are most common. Some pairs of nations compete against one another for a perpetual trophy. If a Series between two such nations is drawn, the holder of the trophy retains it.

Non-Test first class cricket differs from Test cricket in only a few respects. A non-Test first class match is usually four days long, not five. In a four-day game, the cut-off figure for enforcing the follow-on is 150 or more runs behind the first team. The formula used to determine the minimum number of overs bowled in a non-Test first class match may be different to that used for a Test match;

there is no standard regulation.

Non-Test first class competitions are usually round-robins amongst several domestic teams. Other first class matches include single games between visiting international sides and domestic first class teams.

One-Day Cricket

One-day cricket is a newer concept as compared to test matches. One-day format came into existence only in the 1970's and since then it has become immensely popular. It differs significantly from first class cricket. A one- day

match is played on a single day unlike the test matches. Either a red or a white cricket ball is used, and game can be played under artificial lights.

Each team gets only one innings to play, and that innings is restricted to a maximum number of overs. Usual choices for the number of overs are 50, 55, or 60. However, in modern cricket, a 50-over per side match is played. Each innings is complete at the end of the stipulated number of overs, no matter how many batsmen are out. If ten batsmen are out before the full number of overs are bowled, the innings also gets over. If the first team's innings ends in this manner, the second team still has its full number of overs to score the required runs. The timing of the innings and the break between them are not regulated.

Whichever team scores the most runs wins. A tied score stands. There is no draw result. If the match is washed out, so that the innings are not played, the game is declared a no-result.

In each innings, each bowler is restricted to bowl a maximum number of overs equal to one fifth of the total number of overs in the innings. Either a single new ball is used for each innings, or two new balls, which are alternated between overs. (This is often done with white balls because they wear much faster than red balls.) New balls are never taken during an innings, but replacements for lost or damaged balls are taken as in first class matches.

ONE DAY
  MATCH
BOWLING FIGURES

O M R W
10 2 45 3

In case of rain interruption to the first innings, the number
of overs for each innings is recalculated so that they will
be the same. If rain interrupts the second innings, making
it impossible for an equal number of overs to be bowled,
the number of runs scored by the first team is adjusted to

compensate. There is no standard adjustment formula - it is decided beforehand for any given competition. There are also predetermined number of overs, which must be bowled in each innings for any result to be considered valid; if this limit is not reached the game is a no-result.

Because of the emphasis on scoring runs quickly, wide balls are enforced much more strictly in one-day cricket.

ICC MINI WORLD CUP

One-day competitions are played either as Series between pairs of international teams, round-robin competitions between groups of international teams, or round-robins between domestic teams. A World Cup one-day competition is played between all the Test nations each four years. In recent years, ICC (International Council Cricket) has also introduced Mini World Cup, which takes place every two years.

CHAPTER 15

Bowling Styles

There are basically two styles of bowling: fast and spin. A fast bowler bowls the ball as fast as practicable, attempting to defeat the batsman with its pace, but he keeps in his

mind not to throw the ball. His main motive is to swing the ball in the air, or *seam* it (moves sideways) off the pitch. The swing of the ball makes it difficult for the batsman to play. While a fast bowler has a long run-up, a spin bowler has a more ambling run-up. He uses wrist or finger motion to impart a spin to the ball. The ball then spins to one side when it bounces on the pitch, thus also hopefully making it hard to hit. Fast bowlers generally use the new ball, as it is prone to swing. Whereas a spin bowlers get more spin with a worn out ball. There are also medium pacers, who concentrate more on swing and seam than pace.

A swing bowler holds the seam of the ball at a certain angle, and attempts to release the ball so that it spins with the seam at a constant angle. With one side of the ball polished and the other rough, differential air pressure causes it to swing in the air.

A seam bowler attempts to keep the seam vertical, so that the ball hits the seam when it bounces on the pitch and deflects in its path either to the right or left.

A fast bowler can also pull his fingers down one side of the ball as he lets it go, imparting a small amount of sideways spin to the ball. This can cause the ball to move sideways off the pitch. Such a delivery is called a *leg-cutter*

if the ball moves from the leg side to the off side of a right-handed batsman, or an *off-cutter* if it moves from the off to the leg. A specialist spin bowler can get a lot more spin than a fast bowler bowling cutters, however.

There is two types of spin bowling: *off-spin*, and *leg-spin*. If a bowler twists his hand in a clockwise direction on the release, then the spin on the ball will be such that when it bounces it will spin to his right. This is known as off-spin bowling (so called because, to a right-handed batsman, the ball spins *from* the off side to the leg side). The off-spin delivery itself is called either an *off-spinner* or an *off-break*. An off-spin bowler will sometimes not spin the ball so much, putting more pace on the delivery. Such a delivery is called an *arm-ball*.

Sometimes, the bowler twists the ball anticlockwise and releases it from the palm so that it rolls over the base of the little finger. This gives the ball spin in the opposite direction, so it spins left when it bounces. This is basic leg-spin (because to a right-handed batsman it spins from leg to off). The basic leg-spin delivery is called a *leg-spinner* or *leg-break*.

The interesting thing about leg-spin is that if the bowler cocks his wrist at various angles he can in fact, with the same basic bowling action, produce spin in different directions. With the wrist cocked a little towards the inside of the arm, the bowler can produce *top-spinners*. Go further and the bowler actually ends up producing spin in the same direction as an off-spinner. A ball bowled in this way by a leg-spin bowler is called a *wrong 'un*, or sometimes referred to as a *googly*. Probably trickiest of all is a ball bowled with the hand in the same position as a top-spinner, but released from *under* the hand, thereby gaining backspin. This ball is called a *flipper*.

Therefore, right-handed spinners are classified as: off-spinners, with their simple off-spin and arm-ball deliveries; and leg-spinners, with their leg-spinners, top-spinners, wrong 'un, and flippers.

Leg-spinners cause more problems for the batsman because of the great variety of balls they can produce, but they are generally rarer than off-spinners because it is much more difficult to bowl reasonably accurately with the leg-spin hand action.

A left-hander who bowls with the same action as a leg-spinner is called an *unorthodox* spinner - and these are the rarest bowlers in cricket. The left-handed analogue of the leg-spin delivery (which spins the opposite way, of course) is called an *unorthodox* spinner. The top-spinner and flipper retain their names. And the left-handed analogue of the wrong 'un is called a *Chinaman*.

Let us now classify bowlers according to their bowling speed.

Fast bowler:

130-140 km/h (80-90 mph)

Medium pace bowler:

100-130 km/h (60-80 mph)

Spin bowler:

70-90 km/h (45-55 mph)

Bowlers have a strenuous job to do on the field. With the emergence of one-day cricket, they also make use of the state of the pitch, which is quite crucial to the game, and is one of the things the commentators look at in great detail before the game begins. The nature of the pitch is very crucial in the outcome of the game. Because it's a natural surface, there are usually small inconsistencies in its flatness, hardness and elasticity. Over a multi-day game, or even over a single day, these become more pronounced, so it often gets more difficult for batsman as the game progresses. Spin bowlers have generally found that they get much more spin from an old pitch than a freshly prepared one.

. Some of the different types of balls bowled have special names:

Bouncer:

high. It generally bounces chest height or higher as it passes the batsman.

Yorker:

Yorker is a sort of ball that is pitched very close to the

batsman's crease. A bowler usually bowls it to restrict the batsman from scoring runs and it often gets the batsman out. However, it is one of the most difficult deliveries to bowl. A bowler trying to bowl a Yorker more often than not bowls a full toss making it easy for the batsman.

CHAPTER 16

Batting Shots

The different types of shots a batsman can play are described below:

Block:

This shot is played in a manner by the batsman. It is played with the bat vertical and angled down in the front. While playing this shot the batsman intends to defend the ball rather than to score runs. The ball often drops in front of the batsman and he is not able to score.

Drive:

Drive is an offensive shot played with the bat sweeping down through the vertical. The ball travels swiftly along the ground in front of the striker. A batsman can play an *on drive*, *straight drive*, *off drive*, or *cover drive*. The batsman plays these shots depending on the type of ball the bowler has bowled to him.

Cut:

It is a shot played with the bat close to horizontal, when the batsman attempts to slice the ball. The ball is hit somewhere in the arc between cover and gully.

Edge, or Glance:

It is a shot played off the bat at a glancing angle, through the slips area.

Leg Glance:

Leg Glance is played at a glancing angle behind the legs,

so that it goes in the direction of fine leg.

Pull:

Pull is a horizontal bat shot, which pulls the ball around the batsman into the square leg area.

Sweep:

It is similar to the pull shot, except it is played with the backmost knee on the ground, so as to hit balls, which bounce low.

Hook:

It is played in the same fashion as a pull shot, but played to a bouncer. The batsman tries to hit the ball high in the air over square leg, hoping to score six runs.

French Cut:

It is an attempt at a cut shot, which hits the bottom edge

of the bat and goes into the area behind square leg.

Reverse Sweep:

It is like a sweep shot played with a reversed bat. It is played into the point area.

Most of these shots can also be *lofted*, in an attempt to hit the ball over the close fielders (or the boundary).

The batting strokes are either *Straight bat* and *cross bat*. The straight bat shots are played with the bat held close to the vertical, and are the blocks, drives and glances. Cross bat shots are played with the bat held more horizontally. These include cuts, pulls, sweeps and hooks.

CHAPTER 17

Terms Related With Cricket

Maiden:

It is an over, when a bowler completes it, without conceding any runs from it.

Duck:

A batsman is out for a duck if he is not able to score even a single run.

Golden duck:

A batsman out for a duck while facing his first delivery of the innings is out for a Golden duck. The origin of this term is unclear, but commonly rumored to be because the '0' next to his name on the scorecard resembles a duck egg.

Partnership:

When two batsman score runs together at the crease, it is called partnership. A partnership is very vital for the batting side. There are ten partnerships per completed innings, labelled from *first-wicket partnership* to *tenth-wicket partnership*, in order.

Nightwatchman:

Nightwatchman is a batsman, who comes in to bat out of order towards the end of a day's play in a multi-day game, in order to 'protect' better batsmen. The batting order in an innings is usually arranged with two specialist *openers* who begin the innings.

The main task of the openers is to bat for a while against the new ball. A brand new ball is very hard and bouncy, and fast bowlers can use this to great advantage and can

often get batsmen out. It is very hard to bat against the new ball as it swings and seams. A new batsman is more likely to get out than one who has been on the field and scoring runs for a while.

Now, in a test match, it sometimes happens that a team's innings has only a few men out towards the end of the day's play. If a batsman gets out with about half an hour or less until stumps, the batting captain will sometimes send in a poor batsman next instead of a good one. The idea is that the poor batsman (the nightwatchman) will last for some time and hence protect the good batsman from having to make a fresh start that evening and again the next morning. It is essentially a sacrifice ploy. Of course, it can backfire dangerously if the nightwatchman does get out before stumps. The nightwatchman is a tactic, which is used about 50% of the time when the appropriate situation arises (which itself occurs perhaps once every 4 or 5 games). It just depends on how the captain feels at the time.

Sightscreen:

It is a large screen positioned on the boundary so that it forms a backdrop behind the bowler, so that the striker can see the ball clearly. Sidescreens are white when a red ball is used, and black for a white ball.

Rabbit:

Rabbit is a player (almost invariably a bowler, but sometimes a wicket-keeper) who is a very poor batsman.

Ferret:

Ferret is an *extremely* poor batsman (so called because he 'goes in after the rabbits').

CHAPTER 18

Statistics And Scoreboard

Like all international sports, the game of cricket also has official record books and statistics. There are official records since the time international cricket started many years back. Statistics are maintained for each international player.

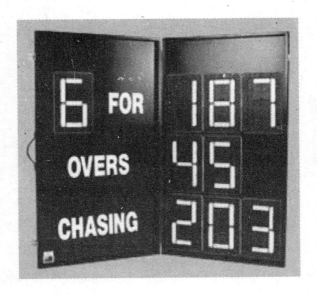

The following statistics are recorded:

Batsmen:

Number of runs scored, time spent batting, number of balls faced, how out (and by which bowler and catcher if appropriate).

Bowlers:

Number of overs bowled, number of maidens bowled, number of wickets taken, number of runs conceded (i.e. scored off his bowling).

Team:

Extras, total runs, wickets fallen, overs bowled, total at each fall of wicket.

A single innings scorecard might look like this:

England: 1st Innings

M E Trescothick c Vincent b Vettori **37**

M P Vaughan c Fleming b Drum **7**

M A Butcher c Astle b Drum **47**

N Hussain c Astle b Vettori **66**

G P Thorpe c Fleming b Martin **11**

M R Ramprakash b Butler **24**

A Flintoff c Drum b Butler **2**

J S Foster not out **25**

A F Giles c McMillan b Butler **10**

A R Caddick c Richardson b Martin **10**

M J Hoggard c Parore b Butler **7**

Extras (b4, lb2, w6, nb22) **34**

Total (397 mins, 88.3 overs) **280**

FOW: 1-26 (Vaughan), 2-6©33 (Trescothick), 3-133 (Butcher), 4-163 (Thorpe), 5-221 (Ramprakash), 6-221 (Hussain), 7-223 (Flintoff), 8-238 (Giles), 9-250 (Caddick), 10-280 (Hoggard).

Bowling: Butler 18.3-2-60-4 (nb10), Drum 24-6-85-2 (nb3, w6), Martin 17-3-58-2 (nb6), Vettori 25-3-62-2 (nb3), Astle 1-0-1-0, McMillan 3-0-8-0.

The abbreviations are:

b. bowled by

c. caught by

st. stumped by

O overs

M maidens

R runs

W   wickets

FOW   fall of wicket

In England, New Zealand, and some other countries the score is given as '(number of runs) for (number of wickets)'. In Australia, New Zealand and some other countries, the score is represented as '(number of wickets) for (number of runs)'.

Bowling figures are sometimes printed in shortened form, for example: Donald 40-5-106-2, Fannie de Villiers 37-7-85-5, etc.

The partnership scores can be seen from the differences between successive fall of wicket scores.

There are some very good performances on field in terms of statistics. A good player can be judged by his capability and talent, but statistics represent the real quality of the player. There are certain criteria that represent the player's caliber. Some of them are given below.

· A batsman scoring 50, or 100, or multiples thereof.

· A partnership adding 50, or 100, or multiples thereof.

· A bowler taking five wickets in a single innings.

· A bowler taking ten wickets in a two innings match. (This is an *excellent* performance and a relatively rare feat.)

· A bowler taking a *hat trick*, i.e. three wickets in three successive balls (perhaps in different overs). This is even more rare.

Each of these tasks is usually greeted with enthusiastic applause from the spectators in the ground and it is a proud moment for the player.

The crowd also usually applauds significant events such as: Any wicket falling, a six, a four, a good over from a bowler (one which the batsmen have great difficulty playing safely), a good athletic effort from a fielder to gather the ball, the innings total reaching a multiple of 50.

The number of runs scored in an innings average about 3 per over for a first class match, and 4 per over in a one-day match. The variation on these numbers can be quite large, differences of up to one run per over being not uncommon.

In a first class match, a captain makes his decision on declaring the innings closed based on the remaining time in the match and the size of his team's lead. He will try to allow as much time as possible to bowl the opposition out, while ensuring they do not have enough time to score enough runs to win.

Over a single player's career, the two most important statistics are:

Batting Average:

It is the aggregate number of runs scored divided by the number of times the batsman has been out. Higher average reflects the better quality of the batsman. It also shows that he has been consistent in his batting career.

Bowling Average:

It is the aggregate runs scored against a bowler divided by the number of wickets taken. Lower average represents better quality of the bowler.

Each of these averages is kept separately for Test cricket, first class cricket, and One-Day cricket. A batting average above 30 is acceptable. A batsman averaging in early and mid 40s is supposed to be good and the batsman, and a batsman averaging in late 40s is considered to be excellent. A batsman averaging above 50 is legendary. Australian batsman Sir Donald Bradman averages more than any batsman in the world. His career average was a record 99.94, far and away the greatest batsman ever to play the game. A bowling average below 25 is considered excellent.

CHAPTER 19

Teams Playing Cricket

The International Cricket Council takes care of all international cricket worldwide. Full members play Test matches.

The test playing nations are Australia, England, India, New Zealand, Pakistan, South Africa, Sri Lanka, West Indies, Zimbabwe and Bangladesh. Bangladesh is the latest entrant in the scenario.

The West Indies is actually an association of Caribbean countries: Barbados; Jamaica; Guyana; The Republic of Trinidad and Tobago; Antigua and Barbuda; St. Kitt's-Nevis; Dominica; St. Lucia; St. Vincent and the Grenadines; Montserrat; and Grenada, Carriacou and Petite Martinique.

The associate members take part in the ICC Trophy. The top teams in this competition also compete in the World Cup. They are currently (with dates of election): Argentina (1974), Bermuda (1966), Canada (1968), Denmark (1966), East and Central Africa (1966), Fiji (1965), Gibraltar (1969), Hong Kong (1969), Ireland (1993), Israel (1974), Italy (1995), Kenya (1981), Malaysia (1967), Namibia (1992), Netherlands (1966), Papua New Guinea (1973), Scotland (1994), Singapore (1974), United Arab Emirates (1990), U.S.A. (1965), West Africa (1976).

Affiliate Members. They are currently (with dates of election): Austria (1992), Bahamas (1987), Belgium (1991), Brunei (1992), France (1987), Germany (1991), Greece (1995), Japan (1989), Nepal (1988), Spain (1992), Switzerland (1985), Thailiand (1995), Vanuatu (1995).

The most famous and the traditional Test cricket Series is The Ashes, played every two years between Australia and

England. The Ashes trophy is a small urn containing *the ashes of English cricket* (in reality the ashes of a set of bails), which *died* in a match in 1882 when Australia beat England for the first time. The Ashes are currently held by Australia, although the physical trophy is kept permanently in a room at Lord's Cricket Ground in London.

The most infamous event in cricket was the 1932-33 English tour of Australia - the *Bodyline* tour. The bodyline has a significant place in the history of cricket. In the bodyline tour, the English team invented a new tactic to confront the strong Australian batting line up. The tactic was to get batsmen out by bowling at their bodies and

placing many fielders in short fielding positions backward of square leg. As the batsmen fended the ball away in an effort to protect themselves, the ball often flew off the edge of the bat into the waiting hands of the fielders, getting the batsman out caught. The English referred to this tactic as *Leg Theory*. The Australians were most annoyed at this theory and named it *Bodyline*.

During this series, several Australian batsmen were injured. Some of the batsman had a torrid time in the middle and were severely injured. The English tactics caused a diplomatic row between the countries. After the tour was over, cricket officials introduced the rules against dangerous bowling, and the restriction of no more than two fielders backward of square leg.

CHAPTER 20

Major Tournaments

The World Cup

With the emergence of one-day cricket it was necessary to have a tournament to decided the world champion.

Fortunately, the notion of one-day cricket was stumbled onto in 1970 and by 1975 the world was ready for a showcase event.

World cup – 1975: Champions – The West Indies

The first edition belonged to the West Indies. After his excellent performance in the Semi Final against England, Gilmour of the West Indies once again took a five wicket haul but the Australians failed to stop Lloyd (Man Of the

Match) from smashing all around a magnificent 102 of 85 balls along with a steady scoring Kanhai (55 of 105 balls) for a 4th wicket stand of 149 runs. Chasing a Herculean task of 292, Australia were 233 for 9 and facing a certain defeat. Thomson (21) and Lilly (16 not out) put on 41

runs (18 short of the target) before Kalicharan bought an end to the spirited 10th wicket fight with a run out. Hence, West Indians became the first World Champions.

World Cup - 1979: Champions – The West Indies

The West Indies ensured their supremacy by retaining the title and defeating England in the final. Man of the Match IVA Richards (138) with CL King's quick fire 86 off 66

deliveries ensured West Indies amass an imposing 286 runs. In reply, JM Brearley and G Boycott built a sound foundation with 129 run first wicket stand before Holding sent both the openers back to the pavilion. Garner completed the formalities with a five-wicket haul to give West Indies a 92 run victory and the title for the second time also.

World Cup - 1983: Champions – India

The bits and bytes cricketers of India handed the Mighty West Indies the most unforgettable shock of their lifetime

in the final. They had a fine and unpredictable run in the tournament. In the final Mohinder Amarnath (26 runs and 7-0-12-3) (Man of the Match) and the superb catch of IVA Richards by athletic Kapil Dev, the Indian Captain, ensured that a small target of 184 was felt like an unreachable top for the formidable West Indies batting line up. India created history by breaking the West Indian monopoly.

World Cup - 1987: Champions – Australia

Reliance World Cup, 1987/88, Final set a clash between the favorites Australia with the Englishmen at sub continent cricket Mecca Eden Gardens, Calcutta on 8th of November 1987. Winning the toss, Australians decided to set the target. Man of the Match DC Boon's steady 75 and MRJ Veletta's fiery not out 45 of 31 balls helped Australians reach 253 in 50 overs. English middle order responded strongly as CWJ Athey (58), *MW Gatting (41) and AJ Lamb (45) helped England reach 246.

World Cup - 1992: Champions - Pakistan

This Pakistani side came from behind to win the World Cup. The Pakistani middle order showed tremendous grit to win the semi final against New Zealand and they carried it on the final. Captain Imran Khan (72 off 110), Javed Miandad (58 off 98), Inzamam-ul-Haq (42 off 35) and

Man of the Match Wasim Akram (33 of 19) played impressively in the final against England.

World Cup - 1996: Champions – Sri Lanka

The Sri Lankans played superbly throughout the tournament basically due to some lusty hitting by Sanath Jayasuriya at the top and a consistent run of batting display by P.A De Silva. The final against Australia belonged to Man of the Match P.A de Silva who earlier helped restrict Australians for 241 runs. MA Taylor (74), R.T Ponting (45)and MG Bevan (not out 36) made some useful contributions. Aravinda set the centre stage bright by scoring 107 and remained unbeaten with Ranatunga (47 of 37 balls) to see Lankans lift their first ever World cup.

World Cup-1999: Champions - Australia

England hosted World Cup after 16 years. The tournament belonged to the Australians who won the tournament after early hiccups under the superb guidance of Steve Waugh. In the final, Man of the Match Shane

Warne bowled superbly (9-1-33-4) to guide his team to victory.

World Cup – 2003: Champions - Australia

The mighty Australians won the World Cup for second consecutive time without losing even a single match in the tournament. In the final against India, Australia scored 359 runs, thanks to a remarkable century by the captain Ricky Ponting and useful contributions from Adam Gilchrist and Mathew Hayden. Indians failed miserably against the strong Australian attack. Hence, Australia deservingly won the tournament.

ICC Mini World Cup

ICC mini World Cup is a biannual event that started in 1998 in the cricket-crazy nation of Bangladesh. In the first edition in Dhaka, South Africa won the tournament by defeating the West Indies. It was a knockout format and was a huge success.

The second edition was held in Nairobi in Kenya in 2000.

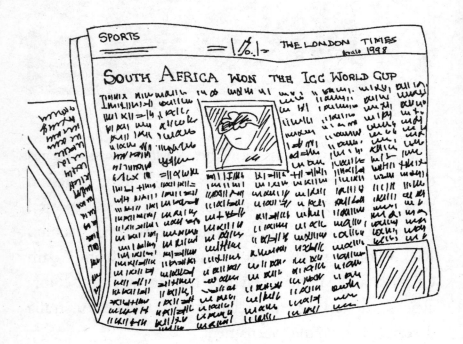

New Zealand won the tournament, largely due to a remarkable century by Kiwi all-rounder Chris Cairns in the final against India. It was for the first time that New Zealand had won any major tournament.

The third edition was the most successful, which was hosted by Sri Lanka in 2002. It was for the first time that a test-playing nation hosted the tournament. The trophy was shared by India and Sri Lanka after a rain interrupted final.

County Championship

Some of the earliest organised cricket matches were between amateur and professional players. From 1806 (annually from 1819) to 1962, the Gentlemen-versus-Players match pitted the best amateurs against the best professionals. Other early cricket matches took place between British universities. The Oxford-versus-Cambridge match, for example, has been played mainly at Lord's since 1827 and became a high point of the summer season in London.

County cricket has been most famous in England. Sussex was the county champion as early as 1827. Gloucestershire dominated the 1870s, thanks to W.G. Grace and his brothers E.M. and G.F. Grace. Gradually, counties such as Yorkshire and Lancashire also famed followed by Kent

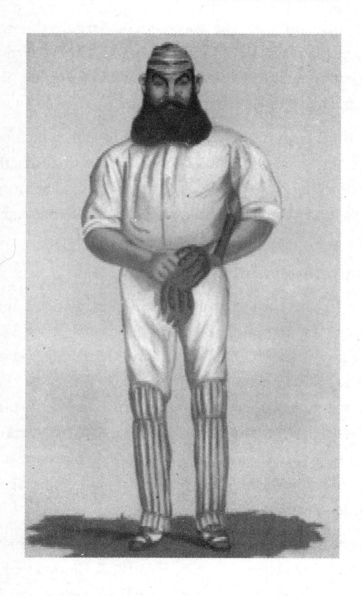

and Middlesex in the 1970s. Later, Middlesex,
Worcestershire, Essex, and Nottinghamshire also came

up.

In the 1960s, the MCC and the counties introduced a One-Day knockout competition (the Gillette Cup—since 1981 the Nat West Bank Trophy) and a separate Sunday afternoon league, which revived public interest.

CHAPTER 21

Indian Domestic Championship

In India, the game has attracted major attention over years. The BCCI (Board of control for cricket in India) is the richest cricket board in India. The major competitions in India are:

Duleep Trophy

The Duleep Trophy competition was started by the Board of Control for Cricket (BCCI) in India in 1961-62 with the aim of providing a greater competitive edge in domestic cricket. The Duleep Trophy was also meant to help the selectors in assessing the form of the cricketers. The original format was that five teams, drawn from the five zones, play each other on a knockout basis. In 1993-94 season, the competition was converted to a league format.

RANJI TROPHY

It was founded as 'The Cricket Championship of India' at a meeting of the Board of Control for Cricket in India in July 1934. The first Ranji Trophy fixtures took place in the 1934-35 season. H.H. Sir Bhupendra Singh Mahinder

Bahadur, Maharajah of Patiala in memory of his late Highness, Sir Ranjitsinhji Vibhaji of Nawanagar, donated the Trophy.

In the main, the Ranji Trophy is composed of teams representing the states that make up India. As the political

states have multiplied, so have cricket teams, but not every
state has a team. Some states have more than one cricket
team, e.g. Maharashtra and Gujarat. There are also 'odd'
teams like Railways, and Services representing the Armed
forces. The various teams are grouped into zones - North,

West, East, Central and South - and the initial matches are played on a league basis within the zones. The top two (till 1991-92), now top three teams from each zone then play in a national knockout competition

If the matches are not finished they are decided on the first-innings lead.

Notes

Goodwill's All About Series

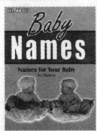

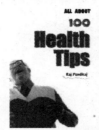

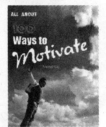

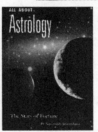

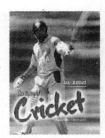

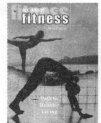

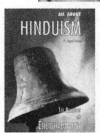

ALL ABOUT
How to improve
grammar
Hone Your Grammatical Skills

ALL ABOUT
How to improve your

Select the right word

CAVE
BOAT
STENCIL
RACE
BABY
PLUM
PULL
PLAIN
DRAW
CLAY

ALL ABOUT
Hypnotism

ALL ABOUT
ISLAM
The Religion of Monotheism

ALL ABOUT   the secret of
magic
Learn to Bewitch

ALL ABOUT
MAGNETOTHERAPY
the Healing
Currents

Harpreet Arora
ALL ABOUT
Marketing Techniques
Be on Target

ALL ABOUT
Meditation
the
Relaxation

ALL ABOUT
Increasing
Memory Power
Sharpen your Brain

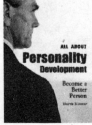

ALL ABOUT
Self
Motivation
Spin the web of Inspiration

ALL ABOUT
Nostradamus
Predicting the Coming Future

ALL ABOUT
Nutrition

ALL ABOUT
Personality Development
Become a Better Person

ALL ABOUT
PHOTOGRAPHY
The Picture Perfect

ALL ABOUT
Reiki

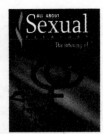

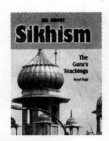

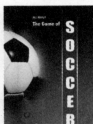